Lost Railways of Galway and the North West
Including
Counties Galway, Leitrim, Longford, Mayo, Offaly, Roscommon, Sligo and Westmeath
by
Stephen Johnson

Ballinamore Station.

Text © Stephen Johnson, 2008
First published in the United Kingdom, 2008,
by Stenlake Publishing Ltd.
www.stenlake.co.uk
ISBN 9781840334302

The publishers regret that they cannot supply
copies of any pictures featured in this book.

Ballycumber Station, 23 April 1955.

Acknowledgements

The author wishes to thank Michele Dunn. The publishers wish to thank the following for contributing photographs to this book: John Alsop for pages 1, 4, 5, 18, 20, 28, 29 and 30 (both); and Richard Casserley for the front cover, inside front cover, pages 2, 6-9, 11-17, 19, 22, 23, 26, 31-34 (both), 35-37, 40, 41, 43, 44 (both) , 45, 46, 48 and the back cover.

INTRODUCTION

The area covered in this book contains much of interest. The Midland Great Western Railway (MGWR) dominated the area with its main lines from Dublin to Galway, Westport and Sligo. The rival Waterford & Limerick Railway (W&LR) made inroads into the MGWR territory with their line from Limerick up through Athenry, Claremorris and Collooney, with running powers from Collooney to Sligo. Although passenger services have ceased on much of the 'western corridor' line, only Limerick to Ennis being served, there is little traffic on the line, but there is an increased interest in the area to provide passenger services. The small village of Collooney once boasted three railway stations, those owned by the MGWR and the W&LR, and a third owned by the Sligo, Leitrim & Northern Counties Railway. From Collooney their line ran to Enniskillen and made a connection with the Great Northern Railway of Ireland (GNR(I)). Livestock was the mainstay of this line until partition took its toll. Natural traffic flows were disrupted and customs checks didn't help as the line crossed the border. Remaining independent throughout its life, it finally closed when the Northern Ireland Government withdrew its support from the GNR(I) and closed the connection at Enniskillen.

Connemara and the northern coast were badly hit during the Famine of the nineteenth century and the Government made attempts at improving transport in the area with a succession of Acts. However, it was the Light Railways (Ireland) Act of 1889 that enabled this area of the country to be opened up. The Act became known as the Balfour Act, after its author, A.J. Balfour MP, the then Chief Secretary for Ireland. These lines were built with Government aid and both a line from Galway to Clifden and Westport to Achill were built under the provisions. As a result, these lines are often known as the Balfour lines.

A number of lines were constructed in the area as a result of an earlier Act, the Tramways Act of 1883. This enabled less heavily constructed railways to be built, often narrow gauge, but running at lower speeds and with special signalling arrangements. An important feature of the Act allowed income for investors to be supported by a Baronial Guarantee which meant that any loss of income was to be made up by local ratepayers with additional help from the Treasury should the amount prove a burden to the ratepayer.

The Cavan & Leitrim Railway was one of the first to propose a railway under these provisions. Although livestock was the initial aim, the line became better known for its coal traffic in later years. In County Clare, the West Clare Railway was built from Ennis to Kilrush and Kilkee. A modernisation programme in the 1950s saw the West Clare become one of the best-equipped narrow-gauge lines running diesel-hauled freight and passenger services. Despite this, the line closed in 1961; it was the last narrow-gauge railway in Ireland.

Our journey through the north-west area of Éire starts with the former Midland Great Western line from Mullingar to Athlone. From here, we travel on a branch off that line from Streamstown to Clara before continuing on from Clara to Banagher on the River Shannon. Moving a little further south, the line from Roscrea to Birr is looked at before travelling west to Attymon and the line to Loughrea. We get on the narrow gauge for the first time in County Leitrim with the Cavan & Leitrim Railway and move on to the Ballaghaderreen branch. Into Mayo, we come to Claremorris, once a busy junction, with its closed lines to Ballinrobe and Collooney. We carry on from Collooney over the Sligo, Leitrim & Northern Counties line to the border at Belcoo. The first Balfour line we come to is the Galway to Clifden line, followed by Westport to Achill. We then move south into County Clare for another narrow-gauge railway, the West Clare from Ennis to Kilrush and Kilkee. We finish our journey by reviewing the closed stations on lines still operating in the area.

Mullingar to Athlone

Passenger service withdrawn	18 May 1987
Distance	27? miles
Company	Midland Great Western Railway

Stations closed	*Date*
Mullingar	Open on the Dublin–Sligo line
Newbrook Racecourse	1962
Castletown	17 June 1963
Streamstown	17 June 1963
Moate	11 May 1987
Athlone Midland	14 January 1985

Mullingar Station looking west, 14 September 1968. The Athlone line is in the foreground and the Sligo line curves away to the right.

This section of line was formerly part of the Midland Great Western Railway (MGWR) main route from Dublin to Galway. The MGWR had built their line from Dublin Broadstone to Mullingar, opening it to traffic on 2 October 1848. Although various schemes had been put forward over the years to reach the west of Ireland, it was the MGWR that were successful in obtaining Acts to do so. The aim was to build to Athlone and then on to Galway. Financial difficulties resulting from the Famine made capital difficult to obtain and eventually the Public Works and Loans Commission were authorised by an Act of 1849 to advance funds. Work commenced in July 1849 and the whole line to Athlone and Galway was opened on 1 August 1851. Intermediate stations were provided at Castletown, Streamstown and Moate. At Athlone, the line had to cross the River Shannon and did so on a 542-feet long, five-span bridge, with one span being able to be opened for shipping. In 1859, the rival Great Southern & Western Railway (GSWR) arrived at Athlone from Portarlington. Although the GSWR had their own station in the town, a connection was made to the MGWR at Athlone East Junction.

J15 Class 0-6-0 No. 198 stands at Mullingar Station on the Sligo line, 11 June 1964.

On 12 November 1852, a platform was provided just over a mile from Mullingar called Newbrook Racecourse; it was for race traffic only and closed in 1962. In the meantime, the amalgamation of the railways in Éire saw the formation of the Great Southern Railway (GSR) in 1924. Changes at Athlone happened a year later when the GSR closed the former GSWR station on 2 March 1925, trains from the Portarlington line using Athlone Midland Station. Fuel shortages caused by the British Miners' strike in 1947 saw a suspension in services from 24 February 1947, although limited accommodation was available soon afterwards on overnight perishable trains. Full services were resumed on 24 March 1947.

K1 Class No. 386 at Castletown Station with the 8.30 a.m. service from Galway to Dublin, 20 April 1955. The K1 and K1A Class were usually capitalise known as Woolich Moguls.

In the 1960s, CIÉ began closing large numbers of small stations around the country, with Castletown and Streamstown becoming victims in 1963. A major change at Athlone occurred in 1985 when Galway trains routed from Dublin Heuston to Galway via Portarlington began using the former GSWR station. The former GSWR station at Athlone was reopened, being more conveniently situated for the town, on 14 January 1985. The former Athlone Midland station closed the same day. Two years later, passenger services on the Mullingar–Athlone section ceased on 18 May 1987, Moate having been closed a week earlier on 11 May. By 2 November 1987, the line had lost its goods service too, but remained open for the occasional special. Although the line is still *in situ*, very few trains have travelled that way over the years.

Streamstown Station, 20 April 1955.

Streamstown to Clara

Passenger service withdrawn	27 January 1947
Distance	7? miles
Company	Midland Great Western Railway

Stations closed	Date
Streamstown	1963
Horseleap	27 January 1947
Clara (MGWR)	2 March 1925
Clara Exchange Platform	1925
Clara (GSWR)	Open on the Portarlington–Athlone line

J15 Class No. 151 pauses at Horseleap Station with an Irish Railway Records Society special to Clara, 18 March 1963.

Clara (MGWR) Station, 18 March 1963.

This odd little line was first proposed in an effort to curb expansion of the Great Southern & Western Railway (GSWR) into Midland Great Western Railway (MGWR) territory. Although an Act had been received in 1857, the MGWR sought to abandon building the line in 1860. However, pressure from local business forced it to be built. The branch opened for traffic on 1 April 1863. Leaving Streamstown, the line travelled south with an intermediate station at Horseleap. Travelling on, the line came to Streamstown Junction, where it joined the GSWR, past the GSWR Clara station, facing Dublin. From opening until 1868, trains arrived at this junction then reversed, or ran round before proceeding back to the station. However, in 1868 the MGWR provided its own station near the junction. Exchange platforms were provided in 1893 to allow an interchange between lines.

Clara (GSWR) Station.

The amalgamation of the railways in 1924 had an effect on the branch's working. In 1925, the Great Southern Railway closed both Clara MGWR station and Clara Exchange Platform, workings reverting to their pre-1868 arrangement. Wartime fuel shortages caused passenger services to be suspended from 8 October 1941. Goods services were suspended between Streamstown and Horseleap on 15 February 1943. A change came on the 22 November 1943 when goods services between Clara and Horseleap were suspended, Horseleap now being served via Streamstown. Horseleap remained served one way or another on account of the spirits traffic the town generated. However, on 24 April 1944, all services were suspended. Goods traffic was resumed on 10 December 1945 with passenger services following nearly a year later on 4 November 1946. This proved to be short lived as the British miners' strike caused more shortages and all services were suspended again on 27 January 1947. In the event, regular services were not resumed on the branch but occasional specials ran until 1959. From 1960 to 1963, the branch was used for wagon storage and the last known movement occurred on 18 March 1963. It finally closed for good on 1 July 1965.

Clara to Banagher

Passenger service withdrawn   24 February 1947
Distance   18? miles
Company   Great Southern & Western Railway

Stations closed	*Date*
Clara	Open on the Portarlington–Athlone line
Ferbane	24 February 1947
Belmont & Cloghan	24 February 1947
Banagher	24 February 1947

Ferbane Station, 8 June 1961.

The first attempt at building a railway to Banagher came in 1861 when the Midland Counties & Shannon Junction Railway received an Act to build a line from Clara, on the Great Southern & Western Railway's (GSWR) Portarlington–Athlone line, to Banagher and on to Meelick. Although work started in 1862, it stopped two years later in 1864 due to lack of funds. After a long delay, with a change of name to the Clara & Banagher Railway and a generous grant from the Board of Works in addition to a Baronial Guarantee, work recommenced in 1880.

Banagher Station, 8 June 1961.

The line opened for traffic on 29 May 1884 and was worked by the GSWR. The branch left the GSWR line one mile to the west of Clara at Clara & Banagher Junction. From here, the line turned southwards towards Banagher with intermediate stations at Ferbane and Belmont & Cloghan. Independence didn't last long and the company was absorbed into the GSWR in 1895. Amalgamation into the Great Southern Railway in 1924 did not have too much effect, but the fuel shortage of 1947 did. Passenger services were suspended on 24 February 1947 with goods following on 10 March. Although goods services were restored on 30 September 1947, passenger services were never resumed.

An interesting development came in the 1950s with the development of the Lemanaghan Bog for cutting sod peat. The peat was transported on a 3-feet gauge railway to a tip head, crossing the branch on a flat crossing. Total closure of the branch came on 1 January 1963.

Roscrea to Birr

Passenger service withdrawn	1 January 1963
Distance	11? miles
Company	Midland Great Western Railway

Stations closed	*Date*
Roscrea	Open on the Ballybrophy–Limerick line
Brosna Halt	1 January 1963
Birr *	1 January 1963

* Originally named Parsonstown; renamed February 1900.

Brosna Halt, 23 April 1953.

Various proposals for a line to Limerick had been made over the years, but in the event the route chosen was from Ballybrophy on the Great Southern & Western Railway's (GSWR) Dublin–Cork line via Roscrea, Nenagh and joining the Limerick & Castleconnell Railway at Birdhill. The initial section of line was authorised in 1854 as the Roscrea & Parsonstown Railway. Work commenced and the first section of line from Ballybrophy to Roscrea was opened for traffic on 19 October 1857. The Roscrea to Parsonstown section was opened for traffic on 8 March 1858. When the next section of the Limerick line was built, the junction was made at Roscrea, leaving Parsonstown on a branch. Further developments occurred at Parsonstown with the building of the Parsonstown & Portumna Bridge Railway, opening on 5 November 1868. However, this line only lasted ten years and was closed on 29 November 1878. In 1900, Parsonstown became known as Birr by local request. An intermediate station, Brosna Halt, was opened in 1910.

Fuel shortages caused by the British miners' strike saw passenger services being suspended on the branch on 24 February 1947. Goods services followed a month later on 10 March. As the shortage abated, goods services were restored on 24 May, followed by passenger services on 16 June 1947. Closure of the line came on 1 January 1963.

E2 Class 0-4-4T No. 295 at Birr Station, 24 April 1953. Note the two six-wheel carriages with the birdcage break at the rear.

Attymon to Loughrea

Passenger service withdrawn	3 November 1975
Distance	9 miles
Company	Loughrea & Attymon Light Railway

Stations closed	*Date*
Attymon Junction *	3 November 1975
Dunsandle	3 November 1975
Loughrea	3 November 1975

* Renamed Attymon in the 1970s.

0-6-0 J19 Class No. 610 at Attymon Junction with the 12.30 p.m. service to Loughrea, 7 June 1961.

The town of Loughrea lay on the proposed route of the Irish Great Western Railway of the 1840s, but when this scheme failed in favour of the Midland Great Western Railway (MGWR), Loughrea found itself some miles from the nearest railhead. Although attempts were made to get the MGWR to build a branch to the town, little interest was shown. The opening of the line from Ennis to Athenry in 1869 didn't help matters when a station seven miles to the west was opened called Craughwell & Loughrea. However, in 1883 representations were made and succeeded in 1885 when the MGWR agreed to work the proposed Loughrea & Attymon Light Railway (L&ALR).

Opened on 1 December 1890, the L&ALR attracted a Baronial Guarantee. The line made a junction on the MGWR's Dublin–Galway line at Attymon and a junction station was provided called Attymon Junction. The line continued south with one intermediate station at Dunsandle. Lasting longer than most small concerns, the L&ALR remained independent until 1925 when it was absorbed into the Great Southern Railway. Although threatened with closure from time to time, the fuel shortage caused by the British miners' strike saw passenger services being suspended from 24 February 1947, goods services following on 10 March. Goods services resumed on 24 May 1947 and passenger services on 16 June.

Dunsandle Station, 7 June 1961.

G2 Class 2-4-0 No. 656 at Loughrea Station with a train from Attymon Junction, 21 April 1953.

In 1962, CIÉ employed the use of a small Deutz diesel locomotive to work the branch with one carriage. Although the service seemed assured for the time being, the line eventually closed on 3 November 1975 due to poor traffic levels and increasing costs.

Belturbet to Dromod and Arigna

Passenger service withdrawn   1 April 1959
Distance   Belturbet–Dromod: 33? miles; Ballinamore–Aughabey: 18? miles
Company   Cavan & Leitrim Railway

Stations closed	Date
Belturbet	1 April 1959
Tomkin Road	1 April 1959
Killywilly	June 1888
Ballyconnell	1 April 1959
Ballyheady	1 April 1959
Bawnboy Road & Templeport	1 April 1959
Killyran	1 April 1959
Garadice	1 April 1959
Ballinamore	1 April 1959
Lawderdale	1 April 1959
Fenagh	1 April 1959
Adoon	1 April 1959
Rosharry (2nd station)	1920 (opened 1901)
Rosharry (1st Station)	1901 (opened 1888)
Mohill	1 April 1959
Dereen	1 April 1959
Dromod	1 April 1959
Ballinamore	1 April 1959
Ballyduff	1 April 1959
Cornabrone	1 April 1959
Annadale	1 April 1959
Driney	1 April 1959
Kiltubrid	1 April 1959
Creagh	1 April 1959
Drumshanbo	1 April 1959
Arigna	1 April 1959

A service from Ballinamore at Belturbet Station.

The 8.15 a.m. service from Belturbet at Ballyconnell Station, 15 April 1948.

In 1883, the Cavan, Leitrim & Roscommon Light Railway & Tramway Company Ltd was formed with the aim of exploiting cattle traffic originating from those counties. The original proposal was for a line running from Dromod to Ballinamore and Belturbet. A branch at Ballinamore was to run on to Arigna and thence to Boyle. At the southern end, an additional extension from Dromod to Roosky was envisaged, but in the event this extension was not authorised. Baronial Guarantees were obtained for the Dromod to Belturbet line. Construction started in 1885 and the Dromod to Belturbet line was opened for passengers on 24 October 1887 (goods services had commenced a week earlier). At Dromod, the line had an interchange with the Midland Great Western Railway's Sligo line, and at Belturbet the line connected with the Great Northern Railway.

Dromod Station, *c.*1916.

The Ballinamore to Arigna section opened for traffic a year later on 2 May 1888 and was for a large part a roadside tramway, with the railway suddenly crossing from one side of the road to the other, causing the odd accident over the years. As little of the proposed line in County Roscommon was actually constructed, the company shortened its name in 1895 to the Cavan & Leitrim Railway (C&LR). Beyond Arigna in the Arigna Valley were some coal mines, one of the larger sources of the mineral in Ireland. Although there were a few attempts to extend the line to the mines, nothing was done until the First World War. The Government used powers to build the line and the Arigna Valley Railway was constructed during 1918/19, but didn't open for traffic until 2 June 1920, too late for the war effort. The 4?-mile extension, running through Derreenavoggy to Aughabehy, was the property of the Board of Works and was worked by the C&LR.

Ballinamore Station.

1925 saw the amalgamation of the railways in Éire and the C&LR came under the Great Southern Railway's (GSR) control. The GSR took over the working of the Aughabehy extension until 1929, when the Government leased the line to the GSR at the rate of one shilling per annum. However, the GSR decided to close the section from Derreenavoggy to Aughabehy in 1930, following the exhaustion of the pit. Despite transporting locally produced coal, the line did not escape suspension of passenger services in 1947 due to the British miners' strike. Services were suspended between 24 February and 24 May that year. One interesting feature of the line was the fact that it received a number of locomotives from other narrow-gauge lines around the country over the years. The 1950s looked promising when coal output increased, some of it being used for the cement works in Drogheda and Limerick. This didn't last too long and output decreased again in 1958, resulting in the closure of the whole line the following year on 1 April 1959.

Kiltubrid Station, 19 April 1955.

Since then, the C&LR has been restored by a preservation group based at Dromod. A short section of track has been relayed and was reopened on 27 May 1995.

Kilfree to Ballaghaderreen

Passenger service withdrawn   4 February 1963
Distance   9? miles
Company   Midland Great Western Railway

Stations closed	*Date*
Kilfree Junction	4 February 1963
Island Road	4 February 1963
Edmondstown	4 February 1963
Ballaghaderreen	4 February 1963

Kilfree Junction Station, 8 June 1961.

G2 Class 2-4-0 No. 655 with a train from Kilfree Junction at Edmondstown, 23 September 1960.

The market town of Ballaghaderreen lay some ten miles away from the Midland Great Western Railway (MGWR). Keen to get a railway connection, the Sligo & Ballaghaderreen Junction Railway (S&BJR) was formed, receiving an Act on 13 July 1863. However, nothing much was done and another Act was necessary in 1866 for an extension of time. Despite difficulty in raising funds, construction eventually commenced in 1869 and the line was opened for services on 2 November 1874. The branch left the MGWR at Kilfree Junction, a station being provided there on the line's opening. The line headed south west and an intermediate station was provided at Edmondstown.

Ballaghaderreen Station, 28 June 1939.

The line was worked by the MGWR, but only on a one-year basis. Traffic was so light that the line closed on 1 January 1876. The S&BJR negotiated a deal with the MGWR guaranteeing them against any losses and the line reopened three months later on 24 March 1876. However, the line was not profitable and was sold to the MGWR in 1879. In 1909, a new station was provided at Island Road, some five miles from Kilfree.

Amalgamation saw the line come under Great Southern Railway control in 1924. The fuel shortage caused by the miners' strike of 1947 saw services being suspended between 27 January and 24 May 1947. The branch finally succumbed to closure on 4 February 1963. Kilfree Junction on the main line was closed on the same day.

Claremorris to Ballinrobe

Passenger service withdrawn	1 January 1960
Distance	12? miles
Company	Ballinrobe & Claremorris Light Railway

Stations closed	*Date*
Claremorris	Open on the Dublin–Westport line
Hollymount	1 January 1960
Ballinrobe	1 January 1960

Hollymount Station, 21 April 1955.

The shed at Ballinrobe Station, 24 June 1939.

The small County Mayo town of Ballinrobe had featured in a number of grand railway schemes of the 1840s, including the Connaught Junction Railway and the South Mayo Railway. However, it was not until 1884 that the Ballinrobe & Claremorris Light Railway was formed, with the aid of a Baronial Guarantee and the backing of the contractor Robert Worthington. It took a few years more until an agreement was made with the Midland Great Western Railway to work the line in 1890. Construction went ahead and the line opened on 1 November 1892.

Leaving Claremorris, the branch made its way in a south-westerly direction to Ballinrobe. One intermediate station was provided at Hollymount. The company remained an independent until 1925, when it was absorbed into the Great Southern Railways. Fuel shortages in 1947 saw the suspension of passenger services on 24 February followed by goods services on 10 March 1947. As the situation eased, all services were restored on the 24 May 1947. Now under CIÉ control, the branch only lasted until 1 January 1960 when it was closed completely.

Claremorris to Collooney

Passenger service withdrawn	17 June 1963	Swinford	17 June 1963
Distance	45? miles	Charlestown	17 June 1963
Company	Great Southern & Western Railway	Curry	17 June 1963
		Tubbercurry	17 June 1963
Stations closed	*Date*	Carrowmore	17 June 1963
Claremorris (south)	1 October 1895	Leyny	17 June 1963
Claremorris (MGWR)	Open on the Dublin-Westport line	Collooney (GSWR)	17 June 1963
Kiltimagh	17 June 1963		

Kiltimagh Station, 10 June 1964.

Charlestown Station, 10 June 1964.

This railway was the final part in a long route connecting Limerick to Sligo, in latter years being nicknamed the Burma Road. Claremorris had been reached in 1894 with a station just to the south of the Midland Great Western Railway (MGWR) station. Using the Light Railways Act, two companies were formed to complete the final section, the Claremorris & Swinford Railway and the Collooney & Swinford Railway. The reason for these two companies was that Baronial Guarantees were necessary from two counties, Mayo and Sligo. Even so, the Government still had to make a free grant available to enable the line to be built. However, these two companies did not really exist and it was the Waterford & Limerick Railway (W&LR) that was behind it all with an interest from the Sligo, Leitrim & Northern Counties Railway (SL&NCR). Henry Tottenham, a director of the SL&NCR actually obtained the guarantee from the Grand Jury of Sligo, with the intention of the SL&NCR building the northern part of the line. However, the SL&NCR were not interested and the guarantee was transferred to the W&LR.

Construction commenced and the line was driven northward, making a connection at the MGWR station at Claremorris and on to Collooney, the whole line being opened for traffic on 1 October 1895. The temporary Claremorris (south) station closed on the same day. The railways at Collooney formed an interesting junction. Although the W&LR had their own station, a connecting line was built to join the MGWR and allow trains to run to Sligo. Another connecting line ran under the MGWR line and made a connection with the SL&NCR at their station. In turn, the SL&NCR had their connecting line to the MGWR. So an unusual triangular junction was formed and Collooney boasted three stations. With the opening of this line and the previous extensions from Limerick, the W&LR changed its name to the Waterford, Limerick & Western Railway (WL&WR), reflecting its increased operating area. The WL&WR and GSWR amalgamated in 1901, but not without a few protests from the MGWR who resented the company operating in their area.

Curry Station, 10 June 1964.

Tubbercurry Station, 10 June 1964.

Little changed over the following years apart from the formation of the Great Southern Railway in 1924 and CIÉ in 1945. The British miners' strike of 1947 saw suspension of passenger services on the line between 24 February and 24 May 1947. Events in Northern Ireland saw the closure of SL&NCR on 1 October 1957, the connection to the Claremorris line closing at the same time. The line lost its passenger services on 17 June 1963, all stations closing at the same time. The line continued to be used for freight services for a while until it was closed completely on 3 November 1975, with the connection to the Midland line being severed at Collooney. The odd train did run after closure, the last known movement being in 1988.

Carrowmore Station, 7 June 1961.

Collooney (GSWR) Station.

Collooney to Belcoo

Passenger service withdrawn	1 October 1957	Ballintogher	1 October 1957
Distance	29? miles	Dromohair	1 October 1957
Company	Sligo, Leitrim & Northern Counties Railway	Lisgorman	1 October 1957
		Manorhamilton	1 October 1957
		Kilmakerrill	1 October 1957
Stations closed	*Date*	Glenfarne	1 October 1957
Collooney (SL&NCR)	1 October 1957	Belcoo & Black Lion	1 October 1957
Ballygawley	1 October 1957		

Railcar 2A with the 4.20 p.m. service from Sligo to Enniskillen at Dromohair Station, 18 May 1950.

The Sligo, Leitrim & Northern Counties Railway (SL&NCR) was incorporated on 11 August 1875 to build a line from Sligo to Enniskillen, receiving great support from the Sligo area as it would break the monopoly of the Dublin-based railway companies and give outlets for livestock exports to the north of Ireland and Belfast.

Railcar B at Manorhamilton Station, 18 May 1950.

Glenfarne Station, 18 May 1950.

Construction started at the Enniskillen end and proceeded towards Sligo, with the first section to Belcoo opening in 1879. From Belcoo, the next section to Glenfarne was opened on 1 January 1880. Glenfarne to Manorhamilton opened on 1 December that year while Manorhamilton to Collooney was opened on 1 September 1881. It took another year for the final section of line to be built between Collooney SL&NCR station and the Midland Great Western Railway (MGWR) line at Carrignagat Junction, opening on 7 November 1882 and allowing the SL&NCR access to Sligo via the MGWR line from that point. As described in the previous section, when the Waterford & Limerick Railway arrived at Collooney, a connection line between the two was built running under the MGWR, opening on 1 October 1895. The line was not a financial success and found itself in receivership in 1890. Despite nearly being split and sold to the Great Northern Railway and MGWR, the company managed to pull itself out of receivership in 1897. Another blow came in 1921 with the partition of Ireland. The company operated its line in both areas and, because of this, was exempt from absorption and remained an independent. However, the political change saw traffic flows diverted away from Belfast. Grants were given by both governments to support the line and economies were made. Railbuses were used to replace most of the steam operated passenger services, supplied by the Great Northern Railway of Ireland (GNR(I)). Meanwhile, the GNR(I) was in financial trouble in the 1950s, being supported by both governments. This continued until 1957 when the Northern Government announced closures of large sections of the GNR(I), particularly the Enniskillen line. With a line running to nowhere, the SL&NCR were given no choice but to close, which they did on 1 October 1957.

Galway to Clifden

Passenger service withdrawn	29 April 1935	Ross	29 April 1935
Distance	47? miles	Oughterard	29 April 1935
Company	Midland Great Western Railway	Maam Cross	29 April 1935
		Recess Hotel Platform	1922
		Recess	29 April 1935
Stations closed	*Date*	Ballynahinch	29 April 1935
Galway	Open	Clifden	29 April 1935
Moycullen	29 April 1935		

J18 Class 0-6-0 No. 582 at Moycullen Station with the 4.30 p.m. service from Clifden, 16 July 1934.

Maam Cross Station, 16 July 1934.

Although proposals had been put forward for a railway to Clifden as early as 1866, with one in 1872 obtaining approval, it took until 1890 before a route was chosen and work went ahead. It was the Light Railways (Ireland) Act of 1889 that enabled this railway to be built. Following the Famine, many outlying districts became very poor and were not an attractive proposition for railway companies. Several Acts were passed over the years in an effort to open up these areas to rail communication, but it was the 1889 Act that had the most effect. The Act is often referred to as the Balfour Act, named after its author, A.J. Balfour, the Chief Secretary for Ireland. The Act established the principle of direct state aid by free grants and lines built under this principle became known as Balfour lines.

J18 Class 0-6-0 No. 589 at Clifden Station with the 1.15 p.m. service to Galway, 17 July 1934.

The route chosen was perhaps not the best, following a sparsely inhabited inland route rather than the more populous coastal route. The railway was opened in two sections, from Galway to Oughterard on 1 January 1895 and the remainder to Clifden on 1 July 1895. Worked by the Midland Great Western Railway (MGWR), there were two major engineering features on the line. The first was the 89-yard long Prospect Hill Tunnel at Galway followed by the Corrib Viaduct. The Corrib Viaduct consisted of three 150-feet spans and one 21-feet lifting span for the passage of shipping. Maam Cross station was added a little later in 1896.

Connemara is very scenic and, eager to exploit tourist traffic, the MGWR purchased a hotel at Recess, completely rebuilding it in 1898. In 1902, a platform was added to serve the hotel. However, after the hotel burnt down in 1922, Recess Hotel Platform was closed. Amalgamation in 1924 saw the line coming under Great Southern Railway control and proved to be an early casualty as a result from road competition. The line closed completely on 29 April 1935.

Westport to Achill

Passenger service withdrawn	1 October 1937
Distance	26? miles
Company	Midland Great Western Railway

Stations closed	*Date*
Westport	Open
Newport	1 October 1937
Mallaranny (temporary station)	13 May 1895
Mallaranny	1 October 1937
Achill	1 October 1937

The viaduct and station at Newport.

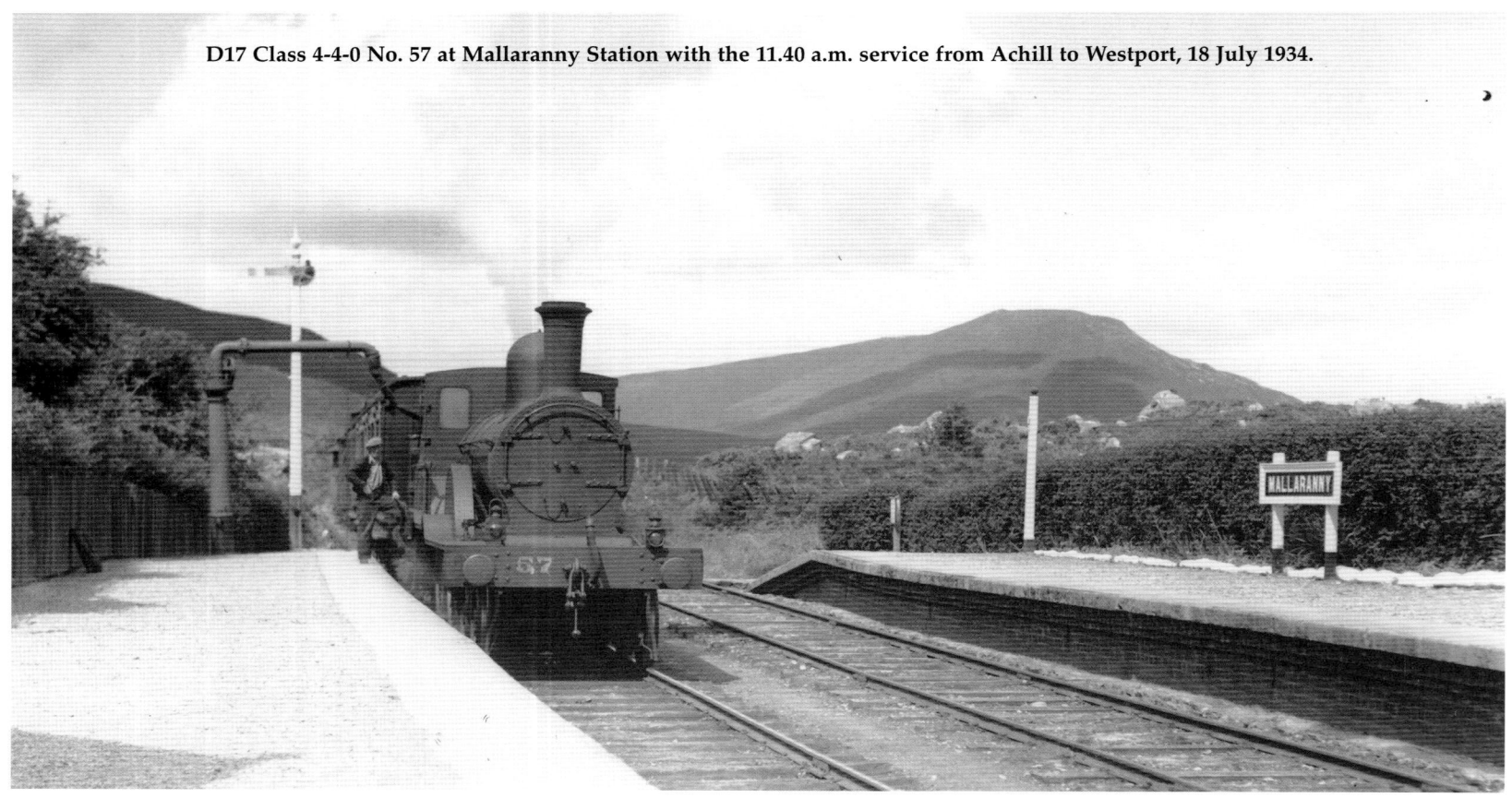

D17 Class 4-4-0 No. 57 at Mallaranny Station with the 11.40 a.m. service from Achill to Westport, 18 July 1934.

The second of the Midland Great Western Railway (MGWR)-operated Balfour lines ran from Westport to Achill. This remote part of County Mayo was subject to a number of schemes with routes suggested from Ballina to Belmullet or from Westport to Belmullet. In 1890, a scheme was put forward to the board of the MGWR and the Light Railway Commissioners, but approval was only given to a line from Westport as far as Mallaranny. In the meantime, Balfour had visited the area in late 1889 and made the decision that the line should be extended from Mallaranny to Achill. Once the decision had been made, work started with the line from Westport to Newport, opening on 1 February 1894, and then to Mallaranny, opening on 16 July 1894. The extension to Achill was entirely Government funded and was built by the Board of Works as the Achill Extension Railway. A temporary terminus at Mallaranny was provided, being replaced by a new station when the extension opened on 13 May 1895. The Achill Extension Railway was handed over to the MGWR upon completion.

Achill Station, 18 July 1934.

There were some major engineering features on the line with a viaduct at Westport and a 133-yard tunnel at Newport, followed by another seven arch masonry viaduct. An 88-yard tunnel was added near Newport in 1896 when a deviation was built from the original route to ease a sharp curve. In 1911, a petrol-engined railcar was used on the mail service and some additional stops were added at level crossings. The railcar lasted until 1916 and had the distinction of being the first vehicle of its type to be used on passenger services. Amalgamation in 1924 saw the line coming under Great Southern Railway control and, as with other Balfour lines, it was an early casualty. The line was closed on 1 January 1935. However, due to the poor state of the roads in the area, it reopened again on 20 May 1936 until improvements could be made to roads. The line finally closed for good on 1 October 1937.

Ennis to Kilrush and Kilkee

Passenger service withdrawn	1 February 1961	Miltown Malbay	1 February 1961
Distance	48 miles	Quilty	1 February 1961
Company	West Clare Railway	Kilmurray	1 February 1961
		Craggaknock	1 February 1961
Stations closed	*Date*	Doonbeg	1 February 1961
Ennis	Open on line to Limerick	Shragh	1 February 1961
Lifford	1 February 1961	Moyasta Junction	1 February 1961
Ruane *	1 February 1961	Blackweir	1 February 1961
Corofin	1 February 1961	Kilkee	1 February 1961
Roxton **	Date unknown	Moyasta Junction	1 February 1961
Willbrook	1 February 1961	Moyasta Loop Platform	by 1954
Clouna	1 February 1961	Kilrush	1 February 1961
Monreal	1 February 1961	Cappagh Pier	1916
Ennistymon	1 February 1961		
Workhouse	1 February 1961	* Originally Ruan; renamed Ruane 5 May 1952.	
Lahinch ***	1 February 1961	** Station here in early years.	
Hanrahan's Bridge	1 February 1961	*** Called Lehinch until *c.*1900	
Rineen	1 February 1961		

There were a few abortive attempts at building railways in Co. Clare, with one broad gauge scheme coming to nothing in 1860 followed by another in 1862. The Ennis & West Clare Railway was authorised in 1871 and although it was not built, it was the first narrow-gauge railway to be approved and its course was similar to the later West Clare route. Changes in railway regulations with the 1883 Tramways Act, however, permitted another company - the West Clare Railway - to be formed in 1884, supported by Baronial Guarantees. Built as a 3-feet narrow-gauge railway, the West Clare left Ennis, where it had a connection to the broad gauge line from Limerick to Tuam, and made its way north west through Corofin before heading west towards Ennistymon and Lahinch. From Lahinch the line turned south, ending at Miltown Malbay. Completed in 1887, the line was opened for traffic on 2 July 1887.

The residents of South Clare were soon demanding a railway connection and a second company, the South Clare Railways, was set up in 1884 to serve Kilrush and Kilkee. Also attracting a Baronial Guarantee, the South Clare continued from the West Clare at Miltown Malbay to Moyasta Junction, where the line divided, the western branch continuing to Kilkee and the eastern branch going to Kilrush. A direct loop from the Kilrush line to the Kilkee line was also built, making Moyasta a triangular junction. The Kilrush to Kilkee section opened for services on 13 August 1892 with the Moyasta to Miltown Malbay section opening on 23 December 1892, although goods trains had been running earlier.

The Atlantic coast of Clare suffers from high winds and in 1897 and 1899 trains were blown over during gales. Measures were taken and some carriages were fitted with extra ballast. An anemometer was installed at Quilty in 1911 to measure wind speeds. If the wind speed exceeded 60 mph non-ballasted stock was not to be used and if wind speed exceeded 80 mph, all trains had to stop. Following the formation of the Irish Free State, the Government amalgamated the railways of Éire into the Great Southern Railway (GSR). The West Clare was absorbed in 1925. The GSR experimented with two 30-seater Drewry petrol engined vehicles, but the gradients on the line proved to be too steep and they ended up working the Kilrush–Kilkee line.

Ennistymon Station, 15 July 1934.

Fuel shortages caused by the British miners' strike had their effects here too, causing passenger services to be suspended between 24 February and 24 May 1947. Under CIÉ control, the line was modernised in 1952 with the arrival of four Walker Brothers diesel railcars, similar to the last two purchased by the County Donegal Railway. Additional stopping places were opened and a set of trailer cars were also provided. In 1955, three Walker Brothers diesel locomotives were purchased to take over the goods services. Despite ending up one of the more modern narrow-gauge systems, total closure came on 1 February 1961, making the West Clare the last narrow-gauge system in Ireland.

Dübs-built No. SC 'Slieve Callan', leaving Miltown Malbay with the daily train from Ennis to Kilrush, 25 June 1951.

Bagnall-built 4-6-0T No. 11C at Kilkee Station with a Sunday excursion service from Ennis, 15 July 1934.

Drewry railcar No. 396 stands at the Kilkee Platform of Moyasta Junction.

Since then, a preservation group called the West Clare Railway has been set up, based at Moyasta Junction. A section of line has been laid running through the Kilkee side of the station and was opened for traffic in 1997. The group has also acquired one of the original Dübs locomotives, No. 5 Slieve Callan, that was previously on display at Ennis with the hope of restoring it to working condition.

Stations closed on lines still open to passengers

Mullingar to Sligo

Stations closed	Date
Clonhugh	1947
Multyfarnham	1963
Inny Junction	1947
Street & Rathown	1963
Newtownforbes	1963
Drumsna	1963
Kilfree Junction	1963
Ballysodare	1963

Ballysodare Station, 29 June 1938.

Athlone to Galway

Stations closed	Date
Carrowduff	1963
Oranmore	1963

Athlone to Westport

Stations closed	Date		
Kiltoom	1963	Ballymoe	1963
Nine Mile Bridge	Date unknown	Ballinlough	1963
Knockcroghery	1963	Bekan	1963
Ballymurray	1963	Balla	1963
Donamon	1963	Islandeady	17 June 1963

Portarlington to Athlone

Stations closed	Date		
Geashill	1963	Clara Exchange Platform	1925
Tullamore (2nd Station)	1 October 1865	Ballycumber	1963
Tullamore (1st Station)	3 October 1859	Ballinahoun	c.1940

Manulla Junction to Ballina

Stations closed	Date
Ballyvary	1963

J19 Class 0-6-0 No. 599 at Ballyvary with an afternoon train from Ballina, 20 April 1955.